Life
Begins
at
Seventy

Other books by Gerald G. Hotchkiss

Emily and the Lost City of Ergup

Emily In Khara Koto

Zoe and the Pirate Ship Revenge

Claire at the Crocker Farm

Music Makers, A Guide to Singing in a Chorus

Life
Begins
at
Seventy

Gerald G. Hotchkiss

SUNSTONE
PRESS

SANTA FE

Sunstone books may be purchased for educational, business, or sales promotional use.
For information please write: Special Markets Department, Sunstone Press,
P.O. Box 2321, Santa Fe, New Mexico 87504-2321.

Book and cover design › Vicki Ahl
Body typeface › Baskerville Old Face
Printed on acid-free paper
∞
eBook 978-1-61139-336-1

Library of Congress Cataloging-in-Publication Data

Hotchkiss, Gerald G., 1930-
[Essays. Selections]
Life begins at seventy / by Gerald G. Hotchkiss.
    pages cm
Summary: "Essays about life beyond seventy" -- Provided by publisher.
ISBN 978-1-63293-035-4 (softcover : alk. paper)
1. Civilization, Modern--21st century--Miscellanea. 2. Life--Humor. I. Title.
PS3608.O843A6 2015
814'.6--dc23

                        2014036243

WWW.SUNSTONEPRESS.COM
SUNSTONE PRESS / POST OFFICE BOX 2321 / SANTA FE, NM 87504-2321 /USA
(505) 988-4418 / ORDERS ONLY (800) 243-5644 / FAX (505) 988-1025

Life Begins at Seventy

70

Preface

There is no chronology or order of reading these short essays. You may just open to a page and read on. And should you find a mistake or typo, please be of a generous temperament. In 1631, Barker & Lucas, Charles I's printers, produced an edition of one thousand copies of the Bible, containing a serious mistake. It left out the word "not" in the seventh commandment. In case your Sunday school days are too far gone, it printed "Thou Shall Commit Adultery." If they had not discovered the error, just think of the thousands of marriages that might have been saved.

Confessions: I have never really made the jump from the music I grew up with to rock and roll. It is a disconnect with my children and grandchildren that is truly my fault. No form could continue for more than half a century in order to prove itself. Abstract art falls into the same difficulty. I wonder, is my mind too concrete? Yet I live for the unexplained, the mysteries, the nuances, the shades of meaning in life and art. It is not intended but a fact that many of the titles of these essays are from Broadway. Each great composition has a great lyric behind it. And usually the words came first.

As times goes by, there are too many clocks in my house. When the power goes off, besides the timepieces themselves are those embedded in our refrigerator and stove and telephone, car, you name it, all awaiting a resetting. And my watch has no second hand. No need to see time going by so swiftly.

Where to read: Anywhere, any time, in an armchair or on the throne.

The writer has credentials. For several years I published a magazine called *50 Plus* which was renamed *New Choices*, when the *Reader's Digest* bought it. The first was right on, save for those not ready for that second half of their century, the second just plain foolish. It successfully obscured the truth, but it also successfully obscured what it was all about. The Brits, who face life more squarely, started an older aged magazine with a logo taken directly from the road signs of an aged couple crossing a street. It even ran edited versions of the published obituaries of famous people. Ignoring never say ill of the dead, theirs was a more balanced view of the newly departed. I was a mere lad of fifty-four attempting to tell the senior's story back then; but I am in my eighties now, old enough to know better.

For years, the medical profession separated the mind from the body. Now their brain research has connected the two, as we older folks knew all along. Holding the mind and body together is having a sense of humor. Laughter is cathartic. At our age it is a blessing. Putting a smile on your umbrella relieves a lot of aches and pains. Remember we are no longer wet behind the ears--to mix enough metaphors to make a pundit cry.

Of course, life doesn't begin at seventy, nor did it end at thirty. But we don't have to live in memory lane, just put it in perspective with all the crazy new electronic machines that dominate our world today. And be thankful of the life we lived and are living.

It is said the three demands of a youngster are: see me, hear me, pay attention to me. Well it's clear to those of us in our second childhood that few see us, hear us or pay much attention to us. The world is interested in younger generations. My column will pay attention to us. Not to a seventy-five-year-old Hercules with enormous pec muscles or an aged starlet offering DVD exercises meant for a twenty year old. Just plain us. It will make some fun of our lives because it is a downhill ride, and without some humor at times it is worth less than John Nance Garner's definition of the Vice Presidency.

If you don't know who John Nance Garner was, this may not be for you.

Mirror, Mirror, on the Wall...

Who is the youngest of us all? We go back to a high school or a college reunion, seeking a few friends we haven't touched bases with in fifty years, Boy, do they seem old, much older than us. How come? Now there are differences. Subtract the very wealthy--money helps hide age, and those whose health has so affected looks. Most of us see ourselves fifteen years younger than we are. Compared to our parents at the same age, it is a stretch, but close to the truth. They were at the prime of their lives through the Great Depression and World War II, stressful times that make a difference. We lived for the most part in easy times. But where is that full length mirror in our house?

Since they say youth is wasted on the young, we had better prove them right. Go to a park and sit on a swing if it isn't too low and take a swing. Take off your shoes and put your ankles in the salt water. Read a story to your grandkids. Walk every day. Three miles is great, but two will do. I do the daily newspaper's crossword puzzles, which "ain't" easy for the world's second worst speller. Who is the worst? (I'll tell you at the bottom.) We're still young at heart if we let ourselves be young at mind and body.

Come on, you'll say, are we invisible? When we are pictured in print ads, created by twenty year olds, there we sit in rocking chairs on the front veranda of a lovely farm house or we are nowhere, as a man on TV in a white MD's coat is advising us to take some strange collection of letters ascribed as a remedy to what we don't know but has side affects that include "maybe death."

A few younger people have offered me a seat on the bus or train, which I demur politely, but secretly ask, "Do I really look THAT old?" Or worse, on an airplane traveling alone, a stewardess asked would I mind giving up my legroom aisle bulkhead seat to a lovely young couple who so wish to sit together. I crunched myself into a middle seat far back in steerage and watched that "lovely young couple" never say a word to each other for the rest of the flight!

Rule #1. To hell with any lovely young couple, keep your seat.

When my wife and I go out to dinner, we notice young couples with children. The couples stare at each other while their kids are immersed in iPods or iPads or finger licketedysplit games. We'd rather talk. Then at the end a cup of decaffeinated coffee or to be *au currant* a double espresso. We still can be with it, but...

Rule #2. Never look in a mirror with your glasses on.

But keep them on when you correct the spelling in F. Scott Fitzgerald's notebooks.

"The name is Sousé, accent grave over the e."

Few issues are as disparate in a marriage as humor. What I find hilarious my wife just doesn't get. She loves spontaneous wit and so do I, but jokes and theatrical humor are beyond her. The French writer and art historian, Andre Malraux, defined male humor pretty well. He called it "the study of the absurd actions of the cowardly under stress." We males watch the exaggeration of a fear we studiously hide performed by a comedian, and we're in stitches laughing our own fears out. Or just watching crazy antics. I recall in college at a local cinema seeing "Animal Crackers" and "Duck Soup" back to back. I never laughed so hard in my life. My wife finds Groucho Marx a bore. W.C. Fields, the author of the title of this column, Woody Allen, Mel Brooks, John Cleese keep me sane. Robert Benchley is in a class by himself. "The Treasurer's Report and Other Aspects of Community Singing" is as fine a serious book title as you can find.

The New Yorker is known for its pithy covers. The best need no explanation. Many strike the male heart and leave the female confused. I kept a favorite on the wall of my office at *Look* magazine. It was a scene in a park in the fall. A mother and daughter are dancing over fallen leaves, while the father and a dog, heads down, are lagging behind. My wife asked me to explain it.

There is nothing to dampen a spirit more quickly than to explain a joke.

In the seventies and eighties, I published a magazine very popular with the eighteen to thirty-four year olds, called *Psychology Today*. I discovered that, along with my wife, psychologists and psychiatrists have no sense of humor. The editors planned to run an article entitled "Women Who Menstruate Aren't Fit to be Mothers." I suspected too many readers would take it seriously, but let it run. Low and behold, hundreds of letters from these professionals wrote us explaining the details of the female anatomy.

Not to be disproven, the editors planned a sequel called "The Myth of the Male Orgasm." Perfect for *Mad* or *Playboy* magazine. It ran, and the letters poured in from the same doctors explaining a male's role in conception.

We men are the weaker sex. Humor is essential to our survival, save the psychologists and psychiatrists. They take life too seriously.

I wonder what women think is funny. I know my wife laughs at anything I take seriously.

Of course, there are things I do that my wife doesn't think are funny. Forgetting birthdays or anniversaries or taking out the garbage. She hates dirty words. Our daughters arrived home from college and soon the 'F' word came out, to our surprise. I suggested that we really did not like that word and if they kept using it away from home, it would creep back into our house. Now it seems to be the most popular noun, verb, adjective, adverb and past participle in America. My wife claims it shows a lack of vocabulary in today's youth. I suggest it is a part of the '60s rebellion, along with long hair on boys and no bras on girls. "You think that is funny, don't you?" she added.

Sadly, I don't think the younger generation has much of a sense of humor. Today's *New Yorker* cartoons are banal overworked social satire. I prefer a Peter Arno drawing of a buxom blonde sitting on a bar stool next to an aging bumpkin, who calls out to the bartender, "Fill Her Up!" Just three words. No explanation needed, thank you.

Then there is Political Correctness. Political Correctness is to humor what Prohibition was to drink. Thank the Lord neither works. It is one thing to be physically or verbally abusive to anybody. It is another thing to be able to laugh at our foibles, our follies, our faults and ourselves.

Especially us poor downtrodden men.

PS: I read this column to my wife who said, "I don't think it is funny, and I think it is completely self-serving."

The

How can you give a title of an essay with just one word, "the"? Well, Webster's Collegiate dictionary gives <u>the</u> forty-eight lines of explanation and that's impressive, isn't it? I am referring to the first two definitions, definite and unique. In England and Ireland, I have know two <u>The's</u>. Both hereditary, but in very different manners.

Fred Lecky was The Swanherd of Great Britain, as was his father before him. Swans are a protected bird in Great Britain with all sorts of rules and regulations regarding their protection, including who gets to eat any of them.

Gerald O'Grady was The O'Grady, as was his father before him and his son now. Of course, O'Gradys are not protected in Ireland, but there is only one "The" at a time, and that is protected. Gerald was dashingly handsome, urbane and innocent at the same time, and charming without any sense of entitlement. For we Americans, the very idea that a person is "The" astounds and impresses us, but certainly not Gerald.

Fred was a working-class Englishman living in a brick house on the High Street without a toilet or bathroom inside. The Chairman of ICI, the leading British chemical company, had met Fred and invited him each year to the big soccer matches. Fred was humbled by the Chair without any idea that the Chair was actually in awe of Fred. After all, there are dozens of Chairman, but only one Swanherd, definite and unique.

When I moved to Santa Fe, I was the only Hotchkiss in the phone book for a decade before another arrived with his name added to the book. I was tempted to change my name from Gerald to The. Of course there is no The Hotchkiss, just an old Yankee name from forebears who arrived, certainly not from royalty or even impressive credentials. Nevertheless, I occasionally would sort of like to change Gerald for The in the great Book of Common Names.

A half century ago, somebody in Manhattan created his own country with ambassadors, secretaries, footmen, et cetera, all listed separately in the telephone book. A bit expensive but worth the fun of it.

A close friend who through his old guard family wife was listed in the little black book called The Social Register. Being part Jewish, himself, to keep a distance, he added a son named Felix Frankfurter, in reality his dachshund. At my last reading of a borrowed Social Register, his dog Felix was attending DePaw University.

There are still titles galore in Great Britain and in some European countries. You can even buy some. My favorite is "The Moncrieff of that Ilk," a noble Scotsman. Sir Rupert Iain Kay Moncreiff, 11th Baronet, CVO, QC died in the 1980s, but his eldest son gave the title to a younger brother, The Peregrine Moncrieff of that Ilk, so that he could take his mother's family title as Earl of Errol. Poor Peregrine. Somehow "that Ilk" takes away any distinction of "The."

And I always thought the Earl of Errol was an Aussie named Flynn.

Welcome and Goodbye

Two reporters of *The New York Times*, on leaving their posts in Paris and London, wrote a column about their experiences as outsiders in insiders' towns. I lived in London for more than three years and visited Paris at least two dozen times fifty years ago and have revisited both many times since.

Their comments remind me how very lucky I saw Europe not too long after WWII, but before the New Tate and before too, too many tourists from too, too many countries, all seeking guide books' "must see" all at once. If you could enjoy looking at an oil in the Louvre for seven seconds lest you are encroaching on the couple behind you, you might be able to get a peek at half of all the great paintings in one day. But to be fair, at the V&A in Knightsbridge (Victoria and Albert Museum in South West London) you can still visit all by yourself "the world's largest statute of a rectangulated quadruped." How the *Time's* correspondent claimed to visit that museum and never mentioned this one is beyond me. Curious? It is a large black and white ceramic copy of a mountain of a dog who saved some Lord from a fate worst than death, but that was never explained.

And, therefore, I presume, we are rectangulated bipeds. "I say, Percy, that's quite a toothsome rectangulated biped you dined with last night. Your wife? Pity."

My wife and I were on the top floor of the Musee d'Orsay next to a large clock and overlooking Paris when she overheard one American matron say to her well fed friend, "Florence, now that we've see Toulouse, where do you suppose we can find Lautrec?"

Many of us guys had a first look abroad courtesy of Uncle Sam, but kids today find all sorts of ways to get out of "stateside" early. And what do they do, of course, look for other kids just like them.

We were different. We sought places that were less touristy, more authentic, if we could find them. But both writers describe a hidden but sad theme: most of those unique less known places are gone.

It used to be that, outside of London, in the country, there were dozens and dozens of workmen's and wives' pubs. The pub side for the guys and the salon for the gals. It was their "local." No more. With the highways offering short hops to the country, sophisticated well-healed thirty-something men and women now take a weekend there. The publicans have discovered their spending so bountiful they have spiffed up their establishments, many owned by the big brewers, to cater to these Londoners. And I haven't a clue where the local workers now congregate.

A country workman's pub is where we watched a local in his britches and boots and weathered woolens. As he came in, there was a pause from the stools. He took one and ordered a Best Bitter. After some small conversation, he stood up and sang "Tom Pierce, lend me your gray mare," with a golden baritone that no Metropolitan bass could possibly duplicate. Then he downed his beer.

At the border of Scotland and England, I was introduced to

single whisky cast strength. Unlike blended Scotch or single Scotch, unblended, the cast Scotch is straight out of the barrel at whatever proof it had developed, 120, 140 (i.e. 60% or 70% alcoholic content), as smooth as a whisky can be, but obviously a wee bit more toxic. Next door was an ancient Roman arched bridge under which a small waterfall tumbled among craggy rocks. Just the place for a grown man with two shots of cast strength whisky in his belly to try his mettle crossing the arch. And making it, found a fence that required a return over the same. That's what makes authenticity worthwhile.

Nearby was a part of Hadrian's Wall and the site of a Centurion's Encampment. in which they found a purse with his earnings. Just imagine this well educated civilized Roman surrounded by Celts and Saxons and Blue-bodied Scots in their wolf skins and beehive stone one-room houses. What a difference a thousand centuries make.

Our parents grew up with horses and died with jet travel. We grew up with radio and will die with some advanced electronic instant panorama cell phone that lets us, in our living rooms, zoom down from on high at London right then and there and see a fly on the mane of a Buckingham Palace guardsman's horse.

New authentic, but I'll take mine, thank you.

A Rose is a Rose is a Rose

Books have been written about the joy of gardening, especially in one's retirement years. Not me. My first experience was digging up the dry and worthless soil of Connecticut for a Victory Garden. All our neighbors had one, and it was not competitive like the railway station gardens of England. Every vegetable was nurtured and watered, and we rejoiced in their freshness at dinner. Except summer squash. My older brother and I had less than an appetite for summer squash, so I picked most of their flowering buds, leaving just enough to grow for Mom and Dad.

One winter, my wife's parents rented a house in the Bahamas that came next door to the Duke and Duchess of Windsor. They met him pruning his rose bushes. I guess that's called a touch of royalty.

We left the East for the West years ago just outside Santa Fe, where the land is even less nutritious and hard packed than New England. Of course, that did not deprive my better half of the need for a garden. In fact, she required two gardens, one facing east and one facing west. Flower gardens. To help matters, we put in an underground sprinkling system well before planting. Thus, on top of spading holes for flowers, I regularly cut the underground rubber snakes. Then I dig either side and clean the rubber and go to the hardware store to get connections and connect and tape and replace the snake and cover it up, only to repeat this each year, as she adds flowers to a garden that is already full, thank you, from my viewpoint.

Interspersed in our east garden are two small bushes. Small is a relative word. I was small once, too. Now these bushes are teenagers if not adults. They shade the sun from some flowers, watering from others. So the local pruner is required to clip them, not too much, not enough there, and then add new flowers where the bushes did their dirty-work.

I shall spare you the tale of hanging baskets, the afternoon winds, watering from below and a stepladder.

I call a "chore" that which I am required to do but have little expectation of its worth in my lifetime.

Gardening is unfortunately a renewable life form. Each wee bud needs watering daily. If local bugs take a liking to its leaves, then there is spraying. If yellow bees also take a liking, then there is stinging. If small purple finches like its nectar, then there are droppings. Not on the dainty flowers but on a table or chair.

Some flowers, like tulips, grow straight up for three days, droop for four and then die. I am told they were worth their weight in gold in Turkey. No wonder the Ottoman Empire collapsed. To compensate, there is one, and only one, grand bloomer I willingly cherish. Verbena. It clings to our wall with small white petals whose essence permeates our portal (a patio to you Easterners) and house. Its leaves are green in the summer and barn red in the fall. It never gets the watering it deserves, yet doesn't punish me for my lack of diligence.

We call Paradise the Garden of Eden, but nobody mentions this to the gardener.

Open Up

Easier said than done these days. My manly hands grip a can like a wet washer. Fortunately I have a Gilhoolie, at least that's what we used to call it. It was invented by a dentist in Yonkers, New York, and made by the Edlund Co. in no nonsense Burlington, Vermont. Designers found a Gilhoolie looked too much like a Rube Goldberg, or just maybe too expensive with rotating parts, so whoever makes cap top openers today has simplified it into a long V, with the narrow end for small top and the wide end for large ones.

I much prefer my Gilhoolie, thank you.

Then there are all the foods wrapped in plastic. Some need knives and some need scissors and some need both if you hope to get inside. That would be okay, but how to cut the plastic without cutting what it holds is still a mystery to me.

If the devil is in the details, then he sure loves the quarter-inch-thick plastic that holds utensils, especially anything that includes electric wires and plugs. You can see all the parts, but just try getting them out. Next time I buy one, I'll challenge the cashier to open it for me.

And then there are the CD and DVD wrappers. These companies must be terrified of theft. They so double down on too tight plastic wrappers, you're lucky when you open the CD that its plastic cover doesn't crack. And why the worry about theft? Before watching a DVD flick, you get the FBI and Interpol and the world police warning about being fined $250,000 for copying it. At the same time there are hundreds of thousands of CD and DVD copiers for sale in stores and even on the internet.

And then, my very favorite, the medical pill containers. With their simple, kindly, instructions: push down and turn. Even if you can read the instructions, you push down and turn, push down and turn, or press firmly down and turn--maybe once in four tries the container opens. That's when you learn not to ever close them again.

But RX is being careful that young children don't eat my wife's Diovan. Good for them. When our eldest was under two, my wife bought a small Red Cross medicine cabinet with a safety latch secure from children's prying hands. For the life of her, she could not open it. Turning to put towels away, she watched in horror and amazement as our youngster opened it in a few seconds. Today, our grandkids happen to live hundreds and thousands of miles away. On top of that, my wife has a four-week pill box in which these little critters, the pills, reside, and it is so much easier to open her box than their original containers.

And if she drops one, we have only our fox terrier to worry about.

i Can't Help it

Remember Marlene Dietrich in *The Blue Angel* singing, "Falling in love again, never wanted to. I can't help it." Adding a few years, maybe fifty, I have edited it just a wee bit. One word. "Falling apart again, never wanted to. I can't help it." Adding, "My teeth are leaving me, before their time, no insurance."

For forty years, while gainfully employed, I was covered for eyes, teeth, you name it. Of course, I never collected a dime. My eyes are still almost 20/20, but the teeth have ground to a halt. Root Canals, Partials sound simple. Until the bills arrive.

Sometime ago when he was a New York Senator, after being a Harvard history professor, Daniel Patrick Moynahan was asked, "If you could live in any century which one would you pick?" His answer, terse and to the point, "I really don't care as long as it is after Novocain!"

A friend who lived a lively life until the age of ninety-seven had his teeth removed when he was in his fifties. He said he so hated going to the dentist, he demanded they be removed and was happy ever after. Well, one day he was quite late for a dinner party excusing himself. "I forgot my teeth."

I now have two partials filling the gaps, and I have forgotten them a couple of times, to my wife's chagrin. *No problemo* as they say in Santa Fe. We guys are less concerned with appearance. But hearing aids are a different matter. It is never the fashion issue (seeing the plugs in your ears), it's the effectiveness. Analog or digital, hidden or seen, all they do is amplify with the impossible trick of amplifying who is talking to you, rather than the whole crowd.

I now have greater respect for one of the English Waughs who carried an ear trumpet to debates and other political meetings. When he had heard enough of a speaker, he would look him in the eye and remove his trumpet.

I remove my partials at night, into a glass of blue fizzy water that is guaranteed "to clean and also remove any odors overnight." Odorless teeth? And I always thought halitosis created a gummy smell.

Enough of this. I'll order *The Blue Angel* from Netflix to enjoy the original lyrics, and dream.

What's in Print?

With all the Twitter and Facebook and talk about the usurpation of the printed book by the electronic book, I looked up Mr. Merriam Webster's take on what a book is. (Poor guy, having to live with a first name Merriam.) Anyway, here it is: definition #3, "something that yields knowledge or understanding."

I like the ominous word "yields" as if you have to work a little to find out something. Nobody enjoys working to find out something anymore. We have so many acronyms for things like WMD, why not IG, for instant gratification. Now that's a more enjoyable set of initials and instant, too.

When I set out to write these short comments on the joys of aging, I planned them for a weekly column in newspapers, in the back pages where only the faithful oldsters take or have the time to find them. But alas, I soon learned that the printed newspaper in its constant shrinkage has neither the interest nor money for a pinch of humor as it exists on local, local, local news at best. "Man Bites Dog on East Main Street" sells papers today. You'd read it, wouldn't you?

Yesterday afternoon around four o'clock, Homer Burnside was minding his own business when a mangy cur followed him down East Main Street from the Barber Shop towards Mrs. Grady's Floral Arcade. Annoyed, he turned around, looked at the flea bitten mutt and bit the dog's left ear. Mrs. Pricilla Snoops, staying in the nearby Comfort Inn, saw the incident through her bedroom window and reported it to the police. Burnside admitted he bit the dog and that a flea bit him.

I can't compete with a story like that, although I'd like to know its ending. Was the man fined or did he take the poor mongrel home, give him a wash, put a Band-Aid on his left ear and the two lived together happily ever after.

For a while, when my wife and I lived in London, England (or the United Kingdom or Great Britain, I can't keep the three separate), newspapers never missed the chance to report errant behavior. My favorite was a parson attending a soccer match in Manchester who was caught using his umbrella to lift the dress of an attractive beauty sitting near him. Had I written the leader it would have said: "Peeping Parson Pokes a Petticoat."

Does describing our behavior fit within the bounds of yielding knowledge or understanding? I hope so. Merriam and Homer and Peeping Parson would make my day.

In print or wifi.

"Roll Out the Barrel"

Santa Fe is always listed as one of the most popular places people want to see. But few see what is really special. It is seven thousand feet high and, as such, it is partially high desert and partially sub alpine. With the varieties of animals and vegetation and fish, it is no surprise that the earliest settle-downers, versus hunt and gather and follow-the-herders, came here near rivers, particularly the Rio Grande.

There are literally thousands of sites nearby where these early Americans lived. Archaeologists call them the squash, bean and corn people, their basic foods. They discovered neither metal nor the wheel until the Spanish explorers came in the sixteenth century. Dozens of pueblos exist today with dances and other sacred rituals performed on a regular cycle of planting and harvesting.

Now it seems Canadian archaeologists, studying similar early peoples who, much earlier in the late Epipaleolithic era, became sedentary, claim the first use of grains was to make beer, not stay-in-one place to make bread. They even suggest that in Mexico with the discovery of *tiosinte*, the early mother of maize, it would have been easier to make a local brew than to make a local bread. Ergo, it was possible that a quick buzz came before what to eat.

But to prove it, these archaeologists didn't look in the right places. I'd scour the stone stands around the early ballparks, where they beheaded the winners and losers. I mean, where do we drink our brews in abundance? Look for signs like "Make Mine Mayan" or "A Drink a Day Keeps the Inca Away" or "Tip Back Your Neck for a Slug of Aztec." And dig up their beer bottles, the gourds with the necks cut off.

All we've found for drinking back then was the prize drink of the kings, cacao. You can find recipes for that ancient elixir. It tastes awful. You need a lot of sugar or honey or something sweet to call it fit for a King. But there is no record of *cervesa*. Of course, if they had made an ancient beer, they might have developed the keg and, with the keg, the wheel.

There does not appear to be any early man ballparks in New Mexico, but there is evidence of pre-Columbian rounded pieces of sherds used in playing games. Maybe the predecessors of the casinos erupting up and down the Rio Grande today. With the wheel, spinning around and around from dawn to dusk.

Something's Fishy

"Survey Finds That Fish are Often Not What Label Says" is the title of an article in *The New York Times*. The first label I can remember was "Made in Japan" on some cheap toy or such. Then a canny entrepreneur somewhere out there created a town in Japan called Usa. And, voila! we bought new ones "Made in USA."

Most of us grew up with fresh fruits and vegetables in their seasons, and our mothers cooked them, added spices, and put them in Ball jars for winter dinners. The pressure cooker made it simpler after at least one ingredient popped through the escape valve onto the ceiling. None of us knew where the steaks and roast beefs and lamb chops came from, other than the butcher. And even into the '70s many butchers shot their deer and elk or rabbits and birds and cleaned them themselves for their local produce.

Like everything else in our society, it just took a few miscreants to sell spoiled local foodstuffs, and a ton of lawyers from the big provenders for our government to place Food and Drug regulations that changed everything. There's a move afoot to label each and every food item in the supermarket by its country of origin. A banana from Costa Rica, a jumbo shrimp from Bangalore, New Zealand lamb. But not beef. Apparently, much of it comes from Mexico, after which it sits in the sweltering sun in small pens fattened up on hormones in Texas. And Texans do not want to have to admit the meat's origins any more than they want to admit Darwin was right.

I have only had food poisoning once, in a terrific restaurant in Romania, and who knows what did it. So I do miss local deer or elk or pheasant not raised in pens, but the FDA does fine by me without knowing where these animals and game and fish originated.

Apparently, I am so far behind the curve, as I am with anything electronic, I should just shut up.

Now it seems that labeling by country is really old hat. Labeling itself is under scrutiny. Take red snapper. A nonprofit group called Oceana took samples of a hundred twenty fish labeled "red snapper" and found among them twenty-eight different species of fish, including seventeen that were not even in the snapper family. I've never met the snapper family, but take it there is one.

One explanation given, noted "there are quite simply a lot of fish in the sea, and many look alike." Hardly new--there are a lot of fools on land, and many look alike.

But not surprising, two cities that I usually think of as Honest Abes, Seattle and Boston, provide salmon and cod in each case that is in fact Pacific salmon and Atlantic cod. If you want a terrific book on cod, and I guarantee you'll love it, read *Cod* by Mark Kurlansky.

Anyway, if Mark Twain sounds better than Samuel Clemens, so does Orange Roughy than its true name Slimehead or Chilean Sea Bass than Patagonian Toothfish, (credit due—all this fish info comes from Kirk Johnson).

Somehow, nobody mentions my pet fishy peeve. English sole. It is a delicacy of delicacies, in the piscatorial world second only to Belon #2 Huites, the oysters without comparison. The French Line, on its way from the USA to France, stops midway between England and the continent. Small fishing boats tie up to the ship's bow, and fresh English sole, only found in that channel, are served to the passengers for lunch. It is too delicate to make a voyage across the Atlantic. Shame on every fish counter that offers some sort of flounder under that name.

Well, there is at least one fish story with a character named Archie Leach played by John Cleese. Archie Leach being the original name of Cary Grant. A great story by any other name would not be as good.

That's Life

For years when we lived in the East, my wife and I would see giant buildings being torn down in New York City, where we worked. New ones emerged, and we couldn't remember what was there before. Part of life is moving on, but part is also remembering. We met at *Life* magazine almost sixty years ago when it was the single biggest media in the world. Gone forty years, it is a relic. Like *The Saturday Evening Post* and *Colliers* and *Look* and *Newsweek*. And newspapers all over America. But unlike buildings, we do remember. And miss.

It's ironic that in our youth we were taught that a handshake was absolute. Yet today, nothing is for sure unless it is written on paper, signed and too often requiring a notarization. The fourth estate was necessary to keep the others honest, and the printed word was its signature. With all its emphasis on entertainment, TV may have eclipsed magazines and newspapers in drawing audiences and making huge profits, but is no substitute. It doesn't even try to be one.

An elderly friend, who died at ninety-seven, remembered visiting his grandfather on Riverside Drive in New York and, looking at the

Sunday New York Times, asked "Where are the funnies?" "Let's find out," answered his granddad with a sly smile. They went south a few houses and he was told to ring the bell at another imposing residence. A small man in waistcoat answered and his grandfather asked if Mr. Ochs was in, that Mr. Wurzburger had a question for him. Adolph Ochs, the founder of our greatest newspaper, came to the door and Pete, my friend, aged eight, asked, "Where are the funnies?" Ochs was not known for his sense of humor and briskly answered, "If you wish to see comics, all you have to do is go over to Broadway and purchase one of Mr. Hearst's newspapers." "Do they have the Katzenjammer Kids?" Pete went on, but his granddad moved Pete off the porch and thanked his friend.

Now I remember the Katzenjammer Kids, even thought I had to borrow it from a neighbor because my folks didn't get a Hearst paper on Sunday, just the *New York Herald Tribune*, which had funnies but not my favorite. Today, even the *Times* is having a tough life holding readers, especially younger ones. Yet they have never succumbed, I suppose it is their word for it, to carrying the funnies. The very first introduction to a newspaper for a young tot just learning to read.

Well, that's life, isn't it.

Tally Ho!

My wife and I, upon reading the personals column in a magazine, decided to write one for ourselves. Then we read each other's. We'd already found that other. These exposes of yearnings are rather sad. But a few are rather funny. Take one I read recently in the *New York Review of Books*. It started "NYC Woman With a Sense of Humor, style, and with her own business and a horse..." It's the horse that got me. Many a female describes herself as slim, sexy, adventurous, warm, even emotionally stable, but never with a horse. Usually, she lets you know she has been to Fez, Maracaibo, Beijing, Monaco, Kenya, Pompeii and Uttar Pradesh and seeks a new soulmate who is adventurous and financially stable. I should hope so.

How should I answer the equestrian? Dear g-mail, "In my adventurous life, I once took a rickshaw through the City of New York with a young Russian pulling me. It was his first day on the job and as we entered Sixth Avenue, I told him we needed to be on the west side of the street, whereupon he ran straight across, stopping a bus, two cabs and an SUV in their tracks. However, I do not read the

Style section of *The New York Times*, nor Time Warner's *In Style*, nor do I shop at Bloomingdale's, much less Neiman Marcus. In fact, my favorite shoes have supported my heels and toes for more than thirty years, always with complete sole repairs. My first occasion on top of a horse was at a full gallop during which my seat was always in the wrong place at the right time. After that I found the perfect haven for my family at a ranch in Wyoming where they fell in love with Brandy and Dandy, while I spent luscious hours all by myself with my Sage and assorted flies capturing sixteen-inch rainbows. I am retired from business. Upon this reading, I suspect I really am not the right guy for you. Have you tried E-Harmony?"

Maybe announcing herself as the horse lady isn't as strange as I have presented. E-Harmony and its likes may have developed the most advanced algorithms for matchmaking. But I'll bet horses are not included in the ten thousand characteristics. No, good for you Ms g-mail.

Tally Ho!

Watch the Money

Had I the opportunity of addressing a college graduation class, here it is.

It is the presumption that I address my remarks to you, this graduating class. Offer you my wisdom garnered through years of life expressing the importance of knowing who you are and never failing in that knowledge.

But I do not plan to say those things. Instead I shall be you, each of you. You, through me, will address your parents and grandparents and family and friends attending this graduation ceremony.

Thank you for helping to finance my four years or more stint in getting my degree. I say degree, not education. Not because I did not get one, but because it wasn't the overriding reason I took those years off of my life.

I did this for money.

Before I entered college, I was well aware that college graduates make more money, a lot more money, than high school graduates. I did not tell you this when you saw me as a naïve eighteen year old. No, I saw you as a naïve forty-five or fifty-five year old. Even eighty year old.

And I am not alone. Most of my classmates did, too, and have for decades.

And my college also has, too. Look around you. Who has the best buildings, who pays their faculties the most money, and every year who is adding to their biggest endowment: the Business School, the Law School and the Medical School. Why?

Because corporate CEOs and their ilk, and big law firms and their partners, and doctors with at least one advanced medical degree, especially surgeons, keep on earning much, much more than the rest of you.

I see it in the honors bestowed upon them in later years from their alma maters because they give back so much more money, money well beyond any of their personal needs.

Just look at the last Presidential election. Mitt Romney got more votes from those with a college education than did Barack Obama. Why?

If those college graduates' main purpose was to get an education, to advance their knowledge and understanding of history, the arts, philosophy, ethics, any reasonable person would have bet on Obama receiving their vote.

But he didn't. College graduates are neither craven nor ignorant. They looked at our world and saw it for what it is. They went for the money, and they have succeeded in getting the money, and it should come as no surprise that they voted to protect their money.

And so am I.

Thank you.

Religion

"**N**ever talk about politics, sex or religion" goes the old saying. So let's talk about religion. According to the news, more and more Americans do not identify with any particular religious sect. I don't think it has anything to do with being religious. It has to do with living, not talking about, a good life. Surely, the Nuns and Quakers live a Christian life with little if any fanfare. They are all over the world helping the poor and needy, living among them in seedy, unkempt, sometimes dangerous places.

Anti-Semites talk about Jews and money. But what they never talk about is how Jews use money. They are so much more charitable than any other religious sect, not for themselves but others. It is blasphemous to put them down.

And it is about time we call a spade a spade. If we were politically willing to do so, 90% of our houses of worship would lose their tax exemption as they blatantly tell parishioners who to vote for under the thin veil of "moral issues." When I heard a moderator during the primaries ask each candidate if he or she was a person of

"Faith," I wanted to barf. The implication, of course, was "Do you believe in God?"

Every religion proposes Peace on Earth. And we have the biggest Army and Navy and Marines and Air Corps and Coast Guard and Merchant Marines on earth to prove it. Some call it Pax America after Pax Britannica.

If as many young men and women joined the Nuns and Quakers, a real Peace Corps, as are in our armed forces, maybe we might call ourselves Pax America. And many would die of pestilence and disease and tribal warfare in doing their kind work. But much less than those young men and women who have given themselves in our current wars.

Almost a dozen years ago in Jerusalem, the Holy Center of the three Abrahamic Religions, five senior leaders from each, dressed in their richest finery, Catholic, Orthodox, Islamic, Protestant, Jewish, came together and agreed on one thing. Not peace or love or mercy or justice or humility.

Something more important. "There Will Be No Gay Parade in Jerusalem."

A desire for love of our fellow mankind is in most of our hearts. "Tinkling bells without love" is nothing.

Word, Words, Words

Reading is a very personal thing. Some of us like biographies and histories, some like political science and statecraft, and others prefer fiction. Book clubs offer sharing one's opinion with others. I have found biographies and histories forever being rewritten as the real facts are discovered, usually to the detriment of the too good opinion of a famous person or historical incident. So I prefer fiction. An author's recollection of people and time recreated to make some sense out of life, itself.

Titles fascinate me. I heard tell Jack London bought titles for his short stories. I wonder who thought up *The Call of the Wild*? Then there is a piece of music by Bix Beiderbeck called "For No Reason at All in C." I like that. It fits with James Thurber's *My Life and Hard Times*. Tolstoy's *War and Peace* says it all in three words. Nobody can beat that, except for Melville's opening line in *Moby Dick*, "Call Me Ishmael."

Were I to write a memoir, it might be called *Why I didn't know what I didn't know*. But that's too long. Maybe *Who Cares?* is better.

I have written a young teen novel with an impossible title *Emily and the Lost City of Ergup*. One friend thought omitting Ergup would be better, but I demurred. Without Ergup the title is trite. But it is too long. If I called it *Emily*, a youngster's mother would think it another Jane Austen romance. One story I was challenged by a granddaughter to write was about her, a dog and a pirate. The title was just okay, but the ending superb: "...but that is another story." Well, superb if I write that other story.

I loved *The Three Musketeers* but wondered why the title when the main character is a fourth musketeer. Never cared for *The Hardy Boys*, but every girl read Nancy Drew detective stories. My wife loved all the Oz Books, not just the Wizard, but Glinda and Tic-Tock and Lucky Bucky and Grampa and you name it. "of Oz," perfect for a series written by Frank Baum and I believe one of his children after he died.

Rumpole of the Bailey is another perfect title. John Mortimer's wry wit offers his barrister so many easy ways to make fun and sometimes serious challenges to English law and its practice. Where he got the name Rumpole beats me, but he got it. On the other hand, maybe because I never completed the seven volumes, *Remembrance of Things Past* (or *Á la recherche du temps perdu*, for those of you who know Marcel Proust's French) like the title, left me after the Madeleines.

Make it short and grab the reader. I once drove past a store with a large sign that read "Go Away." Now that was a grabber. I turned around and slowed down to see what it was all about.

A Travel Agency.

You can't beat that.

"That's Entertainment"

When I was seven or eight, I went to the Whalley Theater in New Haven, Connecticut, at two o'clock every Saturday afternoon and saw: two full length features, a Fitzpatrick Travetalks, a Movietone News, as well as Buster Crabbe as Flash Gordon in a thirteen-week serial. For ten cents.

Today, thanks to my seniority, I can see one feature if I don't mind also watching five previews of coming attractions, each more violent and louder than the next, for seven fifty.

Now that's entertainment.

Woody Allen and Mel Brooks are aging, so don't go putting your hopes on too many good old comedies. *Midnight in Paris* could have won the 2012 Oscar, but, of course, comedy isn't considered dramatic enough. Just the tragic part of Janus.

Not that there is no place to be entertained seriously. We have been very lucky. The Metropolitan Opera under the genius of Peter Gelb, even if critics carp on the Ring's staging, now offers us twelve

"Live from the Met's" Saturday Matinee Opera in Hi Definition at theaters all over the world. If you have not seen one, go. If you don't like opera and the crazy, complicated, insane librettos with women playing men and men singing like sopranos, go. If you expect to see three hundred pound gorillas standing still while trilling high Cs, you will be in for a surprise. If you don't have a hankering for Rene Fleming or Anna Netrebko, go see your internist. Or for Jonas Kaufmann, go see your gynecologist.

And then there is Netflix. A chance to see all those thirties and forties and fifties great movies. A private confession. My middle name is Godfrey. As the youngest in a group of cousins and friends, when "My Man Godfrey" came out and I was much too young to swoon over Carol Lombard, I became everybody's butler. "Ooooh Godfrey, bring me a hot dooog!" I hated that flick. It took me close to seventy years before I actually watched it. What I now proudly call "a keeper."

Friends keep up with baseball teams. Not me. Once the players were no longer part of a team but free agents to the highest bidder, I lost my early Yankee or Red Sox passion. Of course, the players have the right to be free, but I always thought of them belonging to a team. You loved yours and hated their closest rival.

Television is another story. At moments it can be everything and more than one could wish for: Neil Armstrong landing on the moon, JFK's funeral, a few great speeches. But its appetite is concentrated on advertising. Whatever gains the largest audience wins the most advertising money. So the most common puerile entertainment pushes out what the original networks were supposed to provide: real news, unabridged news, so we could be an informed citizenry. Even live comedies without canned audience's applause.

Maybe I'm just an old fogey. I loved the "Honeymooners" and the "Sopranos" and all the original "Upstairs Downstairs" and "John Adams."

They were my Idols.

To CD or Not To CD

I am a lifetime member of the before M-something player. I began with 78s, then smaller 45s, and then a tape, and then a cassette, and finally a CD. I have shelves of CDs, from Mozart and Bach to Nat King Cole and Dave Brubeck with Larry Desmond.

Sometimes the early over-played CDs skip, but their biggest problem is their plastic cases. Most have broken one or both edges, so they don't close or easily slip into a CD carrier. Of the newer ones, many have two CDs inside. And it is a life not worth living to discover how many different ways a CD company can configure how to put two CDs in one case.

The most original is the plastic engineer, or rather the engineer of plastic materials, who designed the circular clasp to capture the hole in the middle of the CD. With trepidation I would first attempt to remove the CD by slightly, ever so slightly, bending its outer edges. But it became clear I was about to break the CD, itself. Then I discovered that I was meant to press on the middle of the circular clasp. Like pressing on the top of an aspirin bottle. A few times it popped the CD out, but too often the clasp looked up at me, like my wire haired fox terrier, and didn't give an inch. Finally successful, I had gained half the goal. I was on the fifty-yard line. Now to retrieve the second CD, hidden so secretly somewhere on the right side of my opened case.

This required a wee dram of Scotch before embarking further. I knew that somewhere hidden there was another CD, #2. But how to retrieve it? Did it fold from the outside in or the inside out? Like a rented car when you parked at a gasoline station. Was the tank on the left or right, with sure knowledge when you discovered it, you were parked on the wrong side. CD #2 flipped open, finally appeared, and if #1 was hard to unsnap, just you wait.

My grandchildren have these small M-something sticks holding every pop hit of the last thirty years and The Decline and Fall of the Roman Empire, if they so wished, inside this miracle of infinite smallness. They plug their ears and sally forth inside or outside the house, while I toil, stuck inside by my humongous, their word, CD player.

To CD or not to CD is not the question. But whether tis time to get an M-something and spend the rest of my life trying to figure out how to transfer my CDs onto that little stick, that is the question.

What's in a First Name?

A fact of life of the aging is a tendency, from years of discernment, to make quick decisions. If you have read about making slow and fast decisions, a major work by two Israeli economists, it may be a major mistake to take the fast tract. Nevertheless, with some inherent knowledge that we have fewer years to make mistakes, and a feeling that the years are rushing by much too quickly (and we do know that the time span actually doesn't speed up), we prefer the fast lane.

Example. We grew up with boys and girls named John and Sally and David and Jane and Peter and Barbara. Weird to us are fancy names from historical novels or foreign countries or some aberration from a misspelling of a common name. So we tend to skip novels, even short stories, by these ill conceived nomenclatures. For instance, reading book reviews in a recent *New York Times*, I came across the following: *Out Of The Easy* by Ruta Sepetys, reviewed by Darcey Steinke. About to press on, I decided to read the Darcey review. I do not know the elder Mr. & Mrs. Steinke, but I do wonder why they named their daughter Darcey. If Mrs. loved nineteenth century English novels, why not Emma. Ruta sounds short for an edible bulb.

The novel takes place in New Orleans where the heroine, Josie, the daughter of a lady of easy virtue, is bored by her mother's business and "prefers the local bookstore." Possibly the names may attract a would be young female reader. You may be surprised that this particular book is in "Children's Books" and subtitled "Young adult, ages 14 and up."

At the time of the publication of this book, I have two granddaughters who just make the 14 and up group. And I can imagine a dinner conversation in which one of them says, "Dad, I'm reading a book about a young girl living in a brothel. What's a brothel?" That should choke the mashed potatoes. "Where did you get that book. Who wrote it?" "At the library, from a review by Darcey Steinke and by Ruta somebody."

Had I preferred the slow lane, I would know that Darcey is an in word today. Like a grammar school two granddaughters attended named "Increase Miller," surely a name not to scoff at. And that by early teenage, with hopefully no firsthand experience, both sexes have advanced well beyond stories of the birds and the bees.

In the review, Darcey begins, "As a girl, I was obsessed with prostitutes. The hookers I saw on television..."

Now I never watched "Sesame Street," but I had no idea it took place next to Beale Street in the Big Easy.

"Even educated fleas do it"

How do you write about sex in a family newspaper? The parents will hide it as quickly as possible. The kids will find it within five minutes. And who am I to write about it anyway? What is it? Love and adoration, pure animal lust, curiosity, power, caring, fantasy, anger, relaxation. Social mores restrict several of these emotions or impulses, even if Mother Nature doesn't.

It is serious, yet can be just fun. It is impulsive, yet can be very calculated. It is mutual, but often self-serving.

By this time, your children are bored with this column, so relax.

There are so many books about sex, manuals about sex, novels about sex, jokes about sex, instruments for sex, pills for sex, animal horns for sex, guidelines for sex, religious instruction regarding sex, legal definitions, parental controls, TV limitations, movie restrictions and back yard explanations that it is fair to say.

Whatever it is, it apparently is here to stay and boy it must be really important.

Like all animals, it is an essential part of extending life. Unlike other animals, most of the time we don't even think about that.

Those other times seem to be a terrible concern for some people. Why?

When you find out, please tell me.

The Grocery

$\mathcal{S}$hopping at the grocery store, before it took on high airs and became a supermarket, was so simple and personal. The grocers and butchers had white aprons with smudges of good clean food or meat and a pencil stuck behind their ears to add up what we bought on the brown bag holding our purchases. It's enough that the supermarkets carry everything under the sun, but they change where they place things, just when I used to know where Major Grey's Chutney could be found. Who was this Major Grey, anyway? Did he serve under King Paul's chickens when the British were in the Chinese Opium wars?

Now everything is packaged. I wonder how long that piece of 92% nonfat processed beef wrapped in plastic has been on the shelf. Anyway, I prefer 82% with enough fat to have a taste. And why not call it what it is—a pound of hamburger.

Of course, there are the free groceries. That's what I call the half of sandwiches and salads and other munchies I take home from restaurants. Into the refrigerator, usually somewhere in the back of my Sub Zero. Two weeks later, I take them out and put them in the wastebasket.

The fresh vegetables are numerous, as well as fresh. Should I get lettuce, bibb or romaine, baby spinach leaves or arugula, or boc choy or endive. Now that's a word, pardon my French. Do you pronounce it on-deeve or on-dive?

Then there is Costco and Sam's Club. Terrific buys if you're a family of twenty-five. Trader Joe's has found a great niche with so many wonderful packages for two or even just one. When Whole Foods opened in our town, I marveled at the displayed foods and service. Now I wonder at the prices. Today, everything is organic this and organic that. Pretty soon we'll have organic toilet paper.

I note whether or not the coffee beans come from a village where the pickers are being fairly paid. In Europe everything is labeled with the country of origin. We don't, but maybe that's okay. Just look at the bottles of Extra Virgin Olive Oil on the shelf. They probably come from Italy.

Now, you know even in Italy there can't be that many extra virgins to fill all those bottles.

Ashes To Ashes

Unfortunately, the only rites of passage that we elders know much more about are funerals. We attend them too frequently. If humor's a part of these essays, what's so funny about death? Of course, we are depressed, unless we are just attending to be seen. Or because we have to, not wish to.

Many of us are not regular church or temple goers save for a few special holidays. The latest facts show more Americans commingling their religions in their marriages and many finding their faith in a secular humanism. Quite often, we really don't know our Reverends and they do not know us. They stand before the gathered flock reading parts of the Old or New Testament, offering a formal solace we buy into or not, we sing a hymn or two, and then they try to say something special about a departed they hardly, if ever, knew.

Now that's the deadly part. It is obvious that he or she cannot make up kind words about somebody neither knew. Maybe a relative or friend has told them about the departed. But the comments are stilted, too formal, too placing our loved lost ones in an ethereal goodness far from their true lives. We fidget in a pew, maybe look at our spouse in despair.

And, of course, there is no mention of a foible or unique or funny incident. Our friend is placed in the firmament on high as stable and solid and unreal as an inlaid casket. There is the famous joke of Patty and Mike at the open casket funeral of their friend O'Malley. As the priest gave special praise to the dear departed, Patty said, "Mike, you better go up and take a look, it can't be O'Malley."

Harry Reasoner, the TV newscaster, on the death of Dwight D. Eisenhower, said it best, and I quote a few of his comments.

> "Very few of us are satisfied with funerals. We are often offended by the rhetoric of praise from those who knew our friend less well than we.... It irritates us that someone thinks it necessary to pretend our friend was faultless when faultlessness was not what we loved him for.... We would often prefer to grieve in lonely silence and conduct our own ceremony in private contemplation... funerals are for the living and not the dead and perhaps they are necessary. When they are over, you dry your tears and return to your work, and if there were no funerals there would never be a time to stop crying."

A dear friend died too early in his thirties. He was Episcopalian, his wife Catholic, and she had gone to help in Selma during the riots with a Congregational minister. All three prelates were to speak. His children were young, and one went up front with flowers picked from their garden. That brought out all the handkerchiefs until the priest who did not know Pete commented on his gravitas. Pete had no gravitas and, if he even knew its meaning, would have abolished it. But good for the good Father. The absurdity brought tears of quiet laughter throughout. It was cathartic.

And remember: "Ashes to ashes and dust to dust. If the Camels don't get you, the Fatimas must."

Amen to that.

"It's Not Funny, McGee."

Does a sense of humor change with age? Not the sense, but maybe the humor. Bathroom humor went out when so many of us had more than one bathroom in the house. Not the Brits, of course. Jack Benny played at the Palladium, their big vaudeville theatre. After ten minutes without a response from the audience, he dropped his pants and received an uproar.

I will confess that my beloved Marx Brothers' flicks seem dated and often too obvious. Yet every time Harpo affixes his thigh to a matron's arm, I am in stitches.

With time, we see the same joke or comedic situation updated and repeated. It's not so funny. Yet re-listening to 'Fibber McGee and Molly' I still await the closet opening and the crashing of whatever spills onto the floor and eventually Molly's signature comment, the title of this essay.

We have outlived WWII, Korea, Vietnam and hopefully Iraq and Afghanistan. Five wars are more than enough for any generation. Our attitudes about war have certainly changed. For many of my friends, we still laugh at the same things, our sense of humor unabated. For others, the human toll and toil has hardened them. It is hard to laugh at a story that happens to sit next to a photo of a bloated belly of a famished child or body bags covered with our Stars and Stripes. But I must find something to make me laugh all the more.

A few years ago on a trip to Austria, my wife and I landed in Munich, Germany. Because it was nearby and I wanted to see firsthand a relic of the worst actions of humanity, we visited Dachau. The sheer organization of this death camp was beyond comprehension. At the farthest corner from its entrance, almost hidden, was a small red brick building, the Crematorium. By the time you have walked there, you can hardly breathe. You are beyond hope. But then, in a red circled poster warning, is a sign for "No Smoking." I laughed and cried at the same time. God help a cigarette ash fouling the ovens.

Nobody else seemed to notice the sign they've seen all over the USA. The absurdity and its humor, to me, brought me back to the living.

Mo Udall noted that his best friend in the Senate was Barry Goldwater, the other Senator from Arizona. Their politics were at extremes, but their sense of humor and respect for each other's personal views was a different matter. Any gaffe from one got an immediate witty reply from the other.

What has happened? Look at our congressional houses today. Is there not a difference from taking what you do and believe in seriously and taking yourself too seriously?

Maybe age doesn't change our sense of humor, but the age we live in does.

And That's Not Funny, McGee.

"Dem bones, dem bones, dem dry bones"

We used to know the tibia and fibula and a few also knew the femur. Not anymore. Our knowledge could fill a dictionary of anatomy. The meniscus rips and the fourth vertebra is torn, the retina needs repair and so on and so forth as we sail into the age of Thank God for Medicare. A friend has a luncheon during which anybody who mentions more than one ailment has to put a dollar in the pot for each further complaint.

Another friend of mine, when asked "How are you?" always replies, "Why?" That's a stopper if there ever was one. Of course, when you're told "you're looking fine" the "for your age" is left out. And just as well. How should I look? The "chest out, shoulders back, stomach in" orders of my youth are even more important now. Attention must be paid to my stature not Willy Loman.

Maybe the biggest complaint is from the distaff side as we males refuse to accept a hearing aid. It's not vanity, we're beyond that. These aids, whether analog or digital, whatever that means, are just one step away from the trumpet offering a large cylinder to funnel the sounds into an ear. This is the only industry I know of in health care in which the doctors and the salespeople seem in cahoots in the same office. I must admit when my wife is four rooms away asking me to do something I somehow can't hear her. Especially, "Did you remember to..."

Driving at night separates us not by designated drivers but by who among us can see. Creatures of habit, we continue to have dinner parties after which by nine o'clock our guests are leaving. When one couple gets up, they all do. Why not just have lunches. They can go on until four or five in the afternoon. Maybe one couple might linger on.

As does the sun.

"Just The Way You Look Tonight."

Sunday mornings are my trip through *The New York Times*. Our local paper actually prints the pages, and I go to the National News section to read the obits. To be sure I am not inadvertently there. The paid ones are on the right hand side. I look at the photos and invariably there will be at least one hardly matching the deceased's age. Usually a woman who was once a model or actress. The softness of the tresses catching alluring eyes, a tight chin and lovely neckline. Then, right under the photo the story begins, "94, etc., etc."

Looking at this model's face taken at least seventy years ago, who will recognize the obituary save from photos kept by her children and grandchildren and great-grandchildren, hardly the intended readers. It reminds me of a once famous Hollywood minor star noting that an Italian recently told her, "You must have been so beautiful..." to her chagrin at 88.

It turns out that psychologists have been studying our unconscious biases. Things so ingrained in our early life, they contradict what we perceive of ourselves. One of them is our perception of age. We know we aren't the life of the party any more, nor can we dance all night or do fifty pushups. But these psychologists have a very accurate test of our unconscious beliefs, and 80% of us oldsters deep inside think Age is Ugly. Never mind what youngsters think.

Maybe I am being ungentlemanly towards these obit pictures taken so many years earlier. I have one photo of my wife in her prime that I adore. It catches her energy, smarts, humor, zest for life and beauty all in one unconscious pose. She's still all those things inside, so why not show it outside?

There are men, too, shown in their prime with rugged trim faces. If that's what they wished, so be it. But I suspect most of us would feel it shallow, vain, accepting at the end we're just "old farts," anyway.

Age is many things, too many unpleasant, some full of new joys and unexpected pleasures. Don't ask me to name three. But it isn't ugly. And since all of us, young and old, have taken the same road, undivided, towards growing old, I would suggest to my beloved if she asks me, "What picture of you would you want on your obit?"

I'll say, "Just the way I look tonight."

i Don't Count

Most of the humor for those of us over seventy is black humor. But here's a white one. I was reminded of it recently when on my computer Netflix asked if I would answer a series of questions that would take about ten to fifteen minutes. At the bottom of each page was the actual time my answers took. On question #2, I answered the box asking my age in month and year of birth. When I put down 9/1930, forty-two seconds into the questionnaire, it closed me out. Some might think that was a slap in the face. I guess it was, but enjoyable. Robo questionnaires on the phone do the same.

We don't count except when we vote.

And why would anybody answer these questionnaires anyway. There is no incentive offered. The companies never tell us what they found out. For all I know they sell these answers to other companies for a profit to themselves. My wife likes the obviously political ones. She tries to figure out which party is asking and if it is not hers, she'll make up answers. I wonder how many others do the same. We oldsters are shameless.

The man who started Netflix grew up next-door to a very close friend of ours in Belmont, Massachusetts. Why isn't he interested in the film preferences of those of us who went to the flicks every Saturday without fail. Movies and the radio were our lifeblood. When the lion roared, we roared. We didn't drink a quart bottle of Coke or eat a basket of popcorn, but when the lights dimmed we yelled or whistled and sat on the very same seat every week. We dated in movies, saw all the foreign films before the moving picture came into our homes on TV.

Now we like Turner Classics and Netflix on our flat HD Sony. And to be fair, my wife and I look for films we hope are not full of violence for its own sake. We went to a Cineplex to see *The Hobbit* in 3D, thinking it was such a film, but after ten minutes it turned itself into another shoot 'em up, beat 'em up between monsters.

Maybe he wanted to find out if I would like to stream Netflix on an iPad or an ebook. I always thought a stream was a small river. Maybe he's right.

I don't count.

Spend a Penny

Bathroom etiquette in its vernacular or polite society varies country by country. But none beats the British. Is it embarrassment or just obstinacy, only a Brit knows. The foreigner upon arriving in the realm of kings soon learns what to say and what not to say regarding going to the bathroom. Never say toilet, even a Cockney refrains from such a gaffe. One goes to the loo or spends a penny.

The contraption one discovers does not require a penny. In a pub or hotel it is free. In a department store, it is hard to find. The seat of the toilet, excuse me, the loo, is the same as in the States, but above it is a large ceramic closed tub holding water from which a link chain hangs with a matching ceramic pull at its bottom. This marvel of invention changed England, if not the world, when created by Thomas Crapper. Hence the expression "taking a crap," which no Brit would ever utter. There is an art to pulling that chain, not too quickly nor too energetically. A straight downward solemn pressure, no yanking, will duly send the water to its destination. In the maisonette my wife and I leased, many a female guest spent too long a time in discovery of this art with words I shall not mention uttered in desperation.

Before my future wife arrived in the UK, I lived in digs. That is a short-term rental of an apartment. I took possession of it on an early Saturday morning and found myself needing to spend a penny only to discover there was no toilet paper. In those days, the late 1950s, many shops closed around 11 AM, so I quickly ventured forth to find the paper. Should I not call it toilet paper, but loo paper, spend a penny paper?

I sallied forth to the green grocers, the butchers, a Boots Chemists, a small supermarket to no avail and, as the need advanced, I rushed to the Gore Hotel nearby. Having accomplished my dire need, I found on a table next to the Crapper an unopened box of Jeyes Paper. I took it to the concierge at the hotel's reception and asked if I might buy the box. "I am very sorry sir, but we are not an accredited retailer of toilet tissue," he responded. "Actually, I did not think you were an accredited retailer of toilet tissue," I acknowledged, "but if I left three shillings on the desk and took it would you call a Bobby?' He smiled, "No sir." And I left triumphant.

My immediate joy lasted but the time it took to return to my digs and open the box. Jeyes toilet tissues are squares of waxed paper. Truly and completely waxed on both sides. I am sure they keep one's hands and fingers from the possible chance of being soiled, but their utter destination seemed as impracticable as one might imagine. And was.

Nevertheless, Jeyes took command for the weekend and going to work on Monday I was told that toilet tissue was found at a stationers. After all, crude American, it is paper and paper, of course, is sold at shops that sell paper, stationers.

In fairness to the Brits, at least those not comfortable with Jeyes, normal toilet tissue, as we know it, is also available. In fact, on an excursion to Greenwich, where the yard and the mile is measured and time has its initial beginning, in the loo one finds good soft or near soft toilet tissue. And on each and every square is imprinted "Property of Her Majesty's Government" on each top and "Now please wash your hands" on each bottom.

After all, isn't Cleanliness next to Godliness?

PS: For those of you who prefer exacting truths versus accepted falsehoods, Thomas Crapper did not invent the flush toilet, his company just made better ones. He died in 1910, a late Victorian plumber. He did invent the ball cock still used today. And, in fairness to Jeyes, the earliest usage of the word crap is from the Latin *crappe*, which means chaff, and so it does.

Coming Home

Years ago Clifton Fadiman wrote a best seller named *Why Johnny Can't Read*. It might be updated to "Why Johnny Can't Write." Semi-retired, I worked with a New York museum's magazine and asked the editor why nothing was ever written by the curators. He responded that, years before, the magazine was full of wonderful stories by the curators but now none of them can write.

Some people can still write. Such as this from my insurance company. They discovered that too many terms were not sufficiently explained. And I quote under their revised "DEFINITIONS":

> "Sudden and accidental" Not a defined term
> ADDED A DEFINITION. Defined as an abrupt fortuitous event which is unintended from the perspective of a reasonable person.

I would love a fortuitous event, abrupt or painstakingly slow, but for the life of me cannot comprehend why I would insure myself against such an event. Or even if I were not a reasonable person, which, of course, they do not define. Now I know that law schools have invented new meanings for the common words of the English language, such as "inherent vice." It is under "Losses We Do Not Cover." I can accept that they do not plan to pay for my vices, but even the Ten Commandments, or the original Fifteen that Mel Brooks discovered, do not suggest I shall lust after my neighbor's wife at my birth.

Ah well, I shall have to be resigned to the fact that, should I win the jackpot, they will not pay me a dime for my abrupt fortuitous luck.

I love the written word. I salivate at beautiful writing. And like many of us, watch our language deteriorate in the written and spoken word. My parents told me that on radio in the nineteen thirties you could bet on words properly spoken by announcers and newscasters.

And what do they report today? Felix Baumgartner, a truly heroic jumper, set all sorts of records falling though the sky miles above our atmosphere, staying a life threatening spin, only to land on his feet and walk away from his parachute unharmed in a New Mexican desert. A truly abrupt four-minute fortuitous event.

The New York Times gave him the quote of the day: "It was harder than I expected." I guess editors are so badly bitten they cannot succumb to the more inspirational. Words well phrased, well spoken and worth remembering. Here is what Mr. Baumgartner also said:

> Trust me, when you stand up out there on top of the world,
> you become so humble.
> It's not about breaking records any more.
> It's not about getting scientific data.
> It's all about coming home.

www.ingramcontent.com/pod-product-compliance
Lightning Source LLC
Chambersburg PA
CBHW022016080426
42733CB00007B/620